Kaleidoscope

A Collection Of Poems

Vasanthi Isaacs

Made with ❤ on the BookLeaf Publishing Platform
www.bookleafpub.in
www.bookleafpub.com

Dedication

Dedicated
To
My Family.
My husband,
My daughter,
And
My Grand daughter

Preface

A kaleidoscopic collection of stories, thoughts and observations put together in poetic form to ponder over or delight.
Straight from the heart.

Acknowledgements

Write angle 21 day challenge, Jan 2025

1. Kaleidoscope

A kaleidoscope I did receive,
From my Grandma dear,
I sensed it would be a treat for me,
As her excitement did overflow!
She watched as I with trembling hands
Did set to un wrap my joy!
I opened the bright box within-
And voila! I saw,

A sleek and beautiful telescope
All colorful and gilt edged!
Grand ma ! I yelled and hugged her tight,
You've crowned my pirate life!
Thank you! Thank you! my favorite
And I moved to pirate swag.
'Hush child' she said 'look through the lens',
And I did so with glee;

My jaw did unlock and drop a lot,
As I in awe did gawk,

My tender eyes could scarce take in,
The awesome sight within,
A fascinating feast of color,
A modulating design spinner,
That amazed with each turn of my wrist.
The 'spy glass' erased from my mind.

I turned to Grand ma wonder eyed,
"Just broken glass my child" she smiled,
'And some other tiny things'
Her words did etch upon my heart,
Broken could beauty be.

Now grey and well ahead in years,
All through my life I see,
That broken pieces of our lives,
Through Gods lens and light,
A beautiful vision do become,
An inspiring work of art.

Each bend or twist in our lives,
Does align in beauty fair,
All the broken pieces of us,
We handed over to God,
And gently He does make it all,
A kaleidoscopic thrill.

2. Crooked Smile

Skipping over ropes,
Skipping just for fun,
Skipping to a rhythm,
Skipping to a rhyme.

Memories of joyful times,
Mournful or lazy days,
A muddled mulled overflow,
Of life and loved ones past.

Pushing through the fog,
Of heart aches or deceit,
The feet a willful skip,
Did flip into the trudge.

Soon skipping all the way,
Never missing a beat ,
Faster and happier,
Than many walking by.

When down in the dumps,
Or caught in doldrums,
Add skip to walk if you dare,
Your heart with no care,
Will soon float as a cloud,
And find your crooked smile.

3. Crucible

Lies are believable,
Gossip; desirable,
Reputations; inflammable,
Destruction; regrettable.

All so delectable,
Others' lives; susceptible,
Beware its reversible,
Become your crucible.

All words; accountable,
Truth spoken; auditable,
Life's end; inevitable,
Destiny; irrevocable.

4. Muse Myself

I sat by the sea,
And it's calming waves,
Azure and sapphire green,
Turned to steel and night.
Its waves towered tall,
As a storm did pass,
My muse stood silent,
Un moved through it all.

I wandered into a garden lush,
With fragrant flowers filled,
Foliage verdant, soothing.
Then into halls,
Of great art on walls,
Or orchestral grandeur,
Echoing around,
My muse did sulk unmoved
And sink into silence cold.

I longed to rest my weary head,
In the softness of my comfy bed,
In the quietness of night so still,
While I closed my day in sleep,
She rambled on,
Like a train on a track,
Speedy, unstoppable, electrified,
And set my mind on a whirl.

Till I rose my weary self
And put down all her rhetoric,
Released her pent up exuberance,
Emotions of interactions,
In thoughts and words collected.

Then she was at peace,
And Into dreamless sleep,
She let me slip.
Myself, Muse and I.

5. Soul Connections

As new born s' take their first shocked breath,
And release their loud, clear cry,
As fresh eyes do first search through slits,
And comprehend the light,
As joyful welcome overtakes,
And anxious waiting's done.

As in the days to come,
Many a fight there are,
As to whom baby's favorite is,
A glance, a stare,
A grip, a smile,
In raptures sends the lot!

As in the warmth and love of all,
A new soul its journey starts,
Its' knowing looks does often turn,
To the blackest sheep of all,
And oft flummoxes the cynical one,
Into a believing fool o'er all.

And they forgetting to adulthood grow,
But the one they touched with love,
Cherishes the memory in cynical heart,
As one blind, his white cane does hold,
They remain the visible embodiment,
Of the redemption of his soul.

6. Miracle

Of stars and stardust,,
Shimmering, glowing,
Heavens aura trailing,
In mortals resting,
Quest's fulfilling.

For joy created,
By doubt berated,
Fair havens forgotten,
By chains the immortal,
In mortal woes confined,

Miracle of a smile,
A kind word, a nod,
A courtesy imparted,
A grief in silence shared,
All mortal woes dispel.

Miracles sublime,
Beyond understanding,
By heaven imparted,
In mortals implanted,
Mortal woe's to lift.

Of stars and stardust made
Shimmering aura resting,
Mortal quest fulfilling,
Miracles overflowing,
Miraculous beings made.

7. Gods' Humor

Our Maker's humor,
He twinkling reveals,
For us to witness,
Sometimes, some people,
Unbelievably real.

A bundle of contradictions,
A simile of paradox,
A synergic oxymoron,
A social misanthrope,
A philosopher of mundane.

Confusingly certain,
Clownishly clever,
Carelessly careful,
Cruelly kind or,
Caustically coy.

Angels go scrambling,
Devils minions do hide,
While the maker chuckles,
And His skill reveals,
As a wise old waif,
His will fulfills.

8. Let Me A Dreamer Be

Let me a dreamer be,
Of fairies and elves and pots of gold,
Of incomprehensible universe I see,
Of the mysteries of my mortal life,
Of the immortal within.

Let me wonder at the rainbow,
Its beauty savor,
Not knowing it's an optical phenomenon,
Of refraction, reflection, of water and light,
Or that a ray of light through a prism sent,
Could inverted replicate its hues.

Let me walk barefoot on the grass,
Enjoy the thrill that flows through me,
Not knowing of my circadian rhythm,
And the earths electric field,
My hormones, my sleep, my waking,
Oh please let it be just joy!

Let me my heady morning walk enjoy,
Rest in my spirit and soul,
Not knowing I'm flush with dopamine,
And a serotonin flood,
Or how my walk my maladies doth cure,
As my doc so proudly expounds..

Let me my time with friends enjoy,
As we laugh and prattle away,
Not knowing I'm setting my hormones agog,
And releasing a psychiatrists list,
Or add it to my therapist's chores,
Of things to better me!

Let me a dreamer be,
Along with my fast dwindling tribe,
That walk the tight rope of life,
Knowledge and wisdom balance,
The intangible mysteries that lie,
Beyond the tangible world.

9. I walked A Mile

I walked a mile'
Inside my mind,
Some solace to find.

It took a while,
To find a smile,
Hidden in the mile.

A still small voice,
Did give me poise,
And gently cut the noise.

Clarity did shimmer in,
Feather light, did usher in,
My mind to sleep most kind.

10. Contradictions

The night skies did to golden glow turn,
Siren wails did fill the air,
As nations their wars did wage,
As human lives for 'greater good' paid.

The night skies did to golden turn,
As fireworks of splendor burst,
The cheer of crowds filled the air,
As human lives for' greater good' sang.

In fascination I contemplate,
How we this contradiction face,
Do we our conscience put to death,
A collateral loss of crossfire in mind.

Or are we just puppets and little lives,
Struggling to blend misery and mirth,
Aliens to those with power endowed,
Who in macro, micro lives forget.

Turned to wise old ones of life,
And ancient book of grace to tide,
Wisdom to glean to live and love,
In times of futility and fear.

A candle in your corner be,
Light another fading, faint,
A drop of kindness to parched lips
A river of mercy to unlock.

The smallest service to ones we touch,
In our corner and miniscule life,
Could waves of hope reverberate,
And echo in oceans far beyond.

Thus my contemplation ended,
Contradictions lay suspended,
Striving, striding for peaceful times,
In our days of influence.

Though at times I plagued am,
Of Lady Macbeth's ilk,
Could a thousand rivers' flow,
Our collective souls wash clean.

11. Solitude

Why do we feel pity for one,
Who is left behind alone?
We smile a wish as they pass by,
And after bow and shake our heads,
'How sad and empty is his life,
We say, 'alone without her there'.

I watched him smile and nod as he,
His daily walk did take,
Along the path he walked with her,
A hundred times before,
Somehow I felt he was not alone,
And 'Auntie' accompanied him still,
For sometimes I caught him stifle a laugh,
As if she had whispered a joke.

On visiting him, I did find,
The home was set for two,
As he went in to bring my tea,
I heard him speak to her!

'You've told me many times Rose
That she likes your cookies with tea,
Oh yes! I'll tell her, I'll tell her!
How much you appreciate her!'

I almost fell off my chair 'co s I,
Knew that "Auntie Rose",
Had passed on a few years ago,
Leaving him a grief struck wreck.

He came back smiling with my tea,
Relating his conversation,
And chuckling said she delighted was
When I as a child would pop in for tea
And from the saucer drink.

I rushed on home, all flushed and faint,
My mind a busy whirl,
Aunties' memory did calm me down,
And I pondered about their bond,
How lovely that even death did not
Their lives destroy.

I think they planned it between them,
For the one left behind,
They'd wrap themselves in a blanket,
Of memories made together,
And their remaining days around,
They'd be comfort by the side.

I did not pity him anymore,
I cherished and envied more,
And thought that I was blessed indeed
To witness this love so true,
That neither age nor death could change,
A companionship past life and time,
That thrived in solitude.

12. Whispers

Imprisoned by whispers,
Chained by prejudice,
Surrounded by opinions,
Damned by false praise,
Misunderstood on purpose,
Misinterpreted with cause,
Misconstrued situations,
Miss villain in all.

If hearts could be opened,
So eyes could see,
If minds could be opened,
So ears could hear,
If souls could be touched,
So lips could speak,
Truth and understanding,
Of each other in light.

Good would prevail,
Over captivating bad.

13. Spinning Orb

This blue and beautiful spinning orb,
What chaos she does hold,
Though from afar, she peaceful seems,
And in quiet grace is veiled.

She is a raging inferno,
A powerful magnetron,
A hydro powered dynamo,
In awesome beauty masked.

She deigns the humans to hold sway,
They are a delusional lot,
Ignorant of their fragility,
And her scarce reigned power.

Her patience wearing thin she sighs,
In changing weather systems,
Volcanoes and tornados,
A few floods and tsunamis tossed in.

Moaning and groaning under havoc,
Their ignorance has caused,
Their selfish games of power,
Their careless exploitation.

She waits for the day,
In peace scarcely visible,
When all nature would in harmony,
Thrive and live securely,
And she could to the humans,
Her powers gently submit,
As they with wisdom nurtured,
And her guardians became.

14. Lazarus

"Lazarus come out', he heard,
And felt a blinding light,
He felt the coils of Sheol melt,
And whispering let go.

His friend unveiled as 'Son of God"
And his sisters awaited him,
"Remove his binds and set him free,"
His friend, His Lord did say.

He stumbled, squinting from the tomb,
His tears filled friend to hug,
He did the 'long awaited one' behold,
He on his knees did fall.

His friend's mission he did see,
As bade from far away,
Prepared to play his role as He,
Died and rose again.

He became a living testament,
Of the power of God o'er death,
Crowds did gather as he lived his life,
For his God who called him friend.

The power that made him a miracle,
And removed the sting of death,
Still works a million miracles,
All over the world, we see.

Many a quiet miracle,
We could be passing by,
If only we could pause a bit,
And speak of miracles,
A treasure trove we'd stumble on,
And find our ray of hope.

15. Another Mother

Lost a mother,
Found another,
What an anomaly!

A lucky few,
Find this they say,
Unlucky me no more.

One to me gave birth,
And God in his wisdom took,
Before I hit my terrible teens,
To my father she left my worst.

May be she did a bargain with,
The maker as they discussed,
My many mischiefs and decided,
He would another skilled send.

My dad did heave a sigh as he,
My hand to my spouse did give,
And in heaven my mum,
Did have a smile,
As his mum welcomed me in.

To the world a tough love soul,
I came to know she was,
To me she kind and loving was,
She said she surprised herself.

I spent more years with her ,
Than with my dear departed,
And did find in her a confidant,
Who rooted for my welfare.

We did our differences have,
We were differently made,
But honesty and forthrightness,
Kept us and family together.

She dreaded reaching a 100 years,
And said 'what a bore life is,
I'm tired of waking up each day,
And going about my self'.

'I can't hang around for you child,
Sorry, I'm selfish like that,
Pray to God I'll go soon,
And join the others in heaven'.

She made sure I clearly knew,
That I had made her happy,
That I would have no regrets,
And I would miss her dearly.

God took her as she wanted to,
To the very last detail,
With dignity and grace,
That favors few elderly.

I lost a mother,
Found another
Another one in law.

God often sends a substitute,
If our hearts we did not lock.

16. Cupid Souled

Cupid did pout head down,
Surprised, I asked him 'why/',
He did his doe eyes turn to me,
And say,' I'm out of arrows'.

I laughed and said,
'Not many even fall in love,
These days it's not in fashion
They'd hardly even notice'.

He wailed aloud, and cried a river,
I was quite embarrassed myself,
For all the drama he did make,
For a feeling that was fickle.

He said calming down,
'I'm always misunderstood,
Love is not the end you see,
It is the means to perfect souls!'.

'The human kind are a selfish lot,
Its love that makes them selfless,
And care for another for a while,
Move to greater humors later'.

'I don't blame them much,
Without wings and halos
In mud and mired circles,
No time for them for love and like,
Except if through my arrows'.

I understood then how critical
It was to get his arrows,
For without it all earth would be,
Bereft of souls perfected.

As this great truth did dawn on me,
And I to panic moved,
I found my cherubic friend,
Blushing red and sheepish.

His quiver -filled, replaced,
He whispered shyly "sorry,
I made so many mistakes,
I thought I will not get any.'

'But thank God for selfish man,
Heaven needs me at my job,
To get their souls perfected!',
And off he went with cherubic joy,
To send his arrows flying,
While I in awe did ponder,
His cherubic dalliance,

17. Glass

Glass that's clear,
Glass that's stained,
Glass that makes me,
See things clearly.

A mixture of natures' elements,
Travailed to pristine glory,
A gaffers' gentle breath whispered,
Into delicate marvels molded.

I wonder at its versatility,
Though plenty there's no satiety,
Glaziers stained to divine story,
Or water held to quench the thirsty.

Our lives and times may be creating,
Through gaffers and glaziers passing,
A marvel, a purpose, a work of art,
A stained glass window or,
A glass menagerie of sorts.

18. Morning Walk

Dawning dawn, deep sleep dispelling,
Drawing one's soul to divine times,
Dear Earth seems all anew again,
Day breaks to brand new life and love.

The quiet walk along a path,
Within the stillness of one's soul,
Peaceful steps ever breathing,
Prayers and promises for the day.

I cherish the early morning hours,
Devoid of hustle and bustle,
As parents view a waking child,
Angelic before tantrum day,
God views each one of us,
And the world for a blink
As He meant, seems.

19. Ninja

I am an influencer,
An inspirer of sorts,
Neither my dodgy success,
Nor my faceted mediocrity,
But the sheer stepping forward,
Only the foolish would dare,
Gives courage to some
Hesitating smarts,
Who with skill venture,
Where foolishness trod,
And the world revolves,
By them more blessed.
I am an influencer,
Most clearly defined,
The 'if she can' category,
Ninja of God's glory.

20. Glory Scars

Calloused hands,
A farmers' proof,
When he bountiful
Harvest does bear.

Broken bones,
And twisted sinew,
Many an athlete bears
When victorious stands.

Actors, Singers,
Painters and Writers,
Scars of life do wear,
When by fame embraced.

My heart do not flounder,
Your human trials under,
Their scars and their healing,
Is your call to glory.

21. A Home Among The Stars

A home among the stars,
Way past the Milky way,
In cosmic splendor placed,
Many moon's and sun's away.
A house of sparkling diamonds,
Some amethyst relief thrown in,
Garden of ruby roses,
Blooms of jasper and topaz,
Rich leaves of ethereal emeralds,
Jade and peridot varying hues,
Breathtaking ponds of turquoise,
Seas of sapphire and lapis lazuli,
A sky of shimmering crystal,
Sprays of gold dust at dawn,
At dusk some moon stone showers,
A glowing mist of rest.

While on earth of soil made,
Encased in life and human toil,
Glows the most precious of the universe,
A God given soul to match,
His kaleidoscopic power.